21 Days of November

Rem Sequence

BookLeaf Publishing

Presentation by *BookLeaf Publishing*

Web: www.bookleafpub.com

E-mail: info@bookleafpub.com

ISBN: 9789357696852

First edition 2022

DEDICATION

For Bubby, the reason I keep getting up each day.

PREFACE

30 Days Hath September, April, June and November.

But, for me, November feels like it goes on forever. This month is riddled with memories, feelings and wounds compiled over 40 years. Some people experience seasonal depression in winter. However, mine hits every November, the last month of spring. Like clockwork, I know this will be challenging time, and I brace myself as if against a fierce storm.

This is an opportunity for me to share what goes on at this time for me. It is the first time I have publicly opened my heart at this painful time. If noone sees this, that is ok, because fundamentally, it is an exercise in me bearing witness to myself. Stepping outside of myself to peer within. Stand next to me while I do so.

11.11.2022

Lest we forget
The young men seduced by old men
Who needed their meat to feed war machines
Those who were chewed up, spat out and ground into dust
Returned home as human husks
Anything soft and gentle and able to find beauty
Had been destroyed to protect King and Country
And those husks then made children built of stone
Because how can a husk nurture a small tender seed
When everything feeling and human
Is now in the belly of a war machine?
Lest we forget.

12.11.2022

This morning I stood in the rain
Big juicy drops soaking my naked skin
Thunder rumbling through my bare breast
And as I stared into the sky I realised I was alive.

The time inbetween
The power sucked by the clouds
Which darkened the day
Grew and grew and grew.

Cascading. Snowballing. Amassing.

This afternoon the sky broke
Swollen with water, pressured by air
Flooding the earth, overwhelming all the sad excuses
we have built for drains.
The wounds we have carved in the earth are no match
for gifts from the skies.

13.11.2022

Sometimes the jagged parts of me
Cut through the softness that I have built
To insulate the world from my rage.

And when pushed and pushed and pushed again
I just want to scream
"Leave me be.
Allow me to be broken and suffering in peace."

But all the jagged parts need is to encounter a world
Which is loving. Is gentle. That loves
unconditionally.
This is when the jagged parts don't seem so foreign or
dangerous after all.

14.11.2022

How could I become anyone else?
When I was born into a time where the presence of children
was barely acknowledged
Where our protection and safety was left to two people who
could be good, evil or absent.

Cigarettes were smoked in offices.
You had a phone attached to the wall in your home.
Small children could see topless waitresses in the front bars
of hotels.

And still, you ask why am I am the way I am?
Why do cigarettes make little round holes in your skin?
Why does the sound of a phone ringing peck at your
temple?

15.11.2022

When we start the show
I want you to remember this isn't really me
I am behind the veil
My true form distorted so that I am easier for
you to digest
I speak so you can hear
I move so as not to affect you
I plan ahead so that my presence will not
inconvenience you
You will be comfortable
I will be on fire
You will be charmed
I will be painting false faces
You will think I am fine
While I am dying inside
Or worse, transported elsewhere so that I don't
have to feel the pain of this charade.
I am not even here.

16.11.2022

I crouch down to your level
So you can hear when I speak
Why do I demand such behaviour?
Why do I protect you so fiercely?
Why can't I just let you be?
And in a moment I am disarmed
By deep blue eyes that lock with mine
I fall into them, like I continually fall in love
with you, day after precious day
I forget what I needed to say
Struck by such beauty, I instantly remember
What I need to say to keep you safe.

17.11.2022

Like butterflies floating over grass
Like spring storms emerging from sunny skies
Like two rabbits grooming each other in the evening light
We are all something that has come from nothing.

18.11.2022

I learned at a young age of entanglement
When I saw all the connections
Between people and things and voices and strings
And never knowing exactly why
Nobody saw things as you do.

A butterfly flapping it's wing can cause a hurricane in
Mexico
The rippling builds strength, despite its gentle origins
A word I say can make it's way across the galaxy and
cause a star to implode
Everything touching everything and everyone

Yet. We still feel alone.

19.11.2022

I see groups of people and I wonder
"How do they do what they do?"

20.11.2022

Snow White ate the poisoned apple and
dropped dead
Her soul flew on the wings of a white dove
To deliver the messsage to the Grim Reaper
Finally he could come to collect her,
Please make haste.
His lips touched hers, freedom,
Seated on the Pale Horse
He accompanied her into the realms of
death
A fairy tale ending.

21.11.2022

I hold my hand close
Directly over my heart
Safe loved and ok

When thoughts of never
Rise discreetly from my mind
Safe loved and ok

No more human touch
Scream before I remember
Safe loved and ok

An island alone
Far away from killing fields
Safe loved and ok

22.11.2022

The part of you
That begged to be free
Tied itself back in chains
Because it couldn't sleep without hearing
them rattle.
How tragic it is to be so dependent on your
prisons.

23.11.2022

Time is elastic when I am resting in this place

24.11.2022

I used to be scared of the dark
When I had you, that changed.
Because I realised that
If a perfect human could come out of my body
Then there was nothing I should fear.
There is nothing in the world that should
intimidate me
Or that I should recoil from.
For I am the creator of worlds

25.11.2022

Sterling silver heart
Reminds me of summer love
Swept away again.

26.11.2022

The pain is a stone
Shifting with my beating heart
Find where they connect.

27.11.2022

All flows from my head
Into the space that surrounds
It glows like amber.

I wake in the light
The sun shows many wonders
But the night hides hope.

Night abandons me
I'm the only one who dares
Look beyond the veil.

28.11.2022

My gut still crunches
When I see your deception
Like sheets of cool rain.

To sense you, in life
Not behind the mist of dreams
Would be sobering.

This sack of skin groans
It is meant and blood and bone
Chaos and comfort.

29.11.2022

Your soft gentle soul
Inside a war god's armour
Sings love songs to me.

I, impermanence
You, a trip to the unknown
We, may never touch.

I am at peace now
Time and space collide again
I sit and wait, still.

We draw together
Paths connect and split apart
The grief never ends.

30.11.2022

If your body can spin
Take it out and let it spin.
Let it shriek and flail it's arms.
Let it roll down hills and flip somersaults.
Let it's head fall back and gaze off into galaxies.
Do it now,
Because perhaps there will come a day when it can't.

1.12.2022

The pockets, my son
Hold all the jewels I have sold
To ensure your smile.

When the darkness sighs
I echo it's breath, silent
Not breaking my heart.

Folded within me
I knew your heartbeat, pulsing
I never forget.

I never forget
Warmth of the sun make it so
Reminders of you.

Slumber, my soft child
The armour we wear can wait
For the sun to rise.

You don your chestplate
My being covers you too
Always your shield, sword.

Can I tell you some
Thing you have never heard before?
You know, I love you.